# Popular Ballads Classical Singers

## High Voice

Concert Arrangements by Richard Walters

# Contents

RICHARD RODGERS
- 4    The Sweetest Sounds *(lyric by the composer)*
- 11   I Have Dreamed *(lyric by Oscar Hammerstein II)*
- 19   You're Nearer *(lyric by Lorenz Hart)*

COLE PORTER
*lyrics by the composer*
- 24   I Am in Love
- 33   I Concentrate on You
- 43   I Hate You, Darling

GEORGE GERSHWIN
*lyrics by Ira Gershwin*
- 48   They Can't Take That Away from Me
- 57   Nice Work If You Can Get It
- 65   A Foggy Day/Love Walked In
- 74   Love Is Here to Stay

On the cover: Wassily Kandinsky, *Round and Pointed*, 1930

ISBN 978-0-634-02303-3

HAL•LEONARD®
CORPORATION
7777 W. BLUEMOUND RD. P.O. BOX 13819 MILWAUKEE, WI 53213

Visit Hal Leonard Online at
**www.halleonard.com**

# Arranger's Notes

Among the most fascinating characteristics of standard American popular songs is their amazing ability to retain a distinct identity in a wide spectrum of arranging styles. For this collection I have chosen songs for which I could make appropriate concert settings designed to flatter classical singers and pianists. These are more in the spirit of classical compositions based on the songs, rather than typical arranging.

THE SWEETEST SOUNDS comes from the 1962 musical *No Strings*, a gentle interracial romance that starred Diahann Carroll and Richard Kiley. It was the composer's first stage work after the death in 1960 of his partner, Oscar Hammerstein II, and is the only show in Rodgers' long career for which he wrote his own lyrics. In this instance, the imagery of the words seem to reveal the self-intimacy between Rodgers the lyricist and Rodgers the composer. The result is an unusually chromatic and haunting melody.

I HAVE DREAMED is the famous love duet sung by Tuptim and Lun Tha in the 1951 Rodgers and Hammerstein musical *The King and I*. This love song, sung by two people who have not yet actually become lovers, has similar counterparts in other shows, for instance, "People Will Say We're in Love" from *Oklahoma!*, "If I Loved You" from *Carousel*, "Some Enchanted Evening" from *The King and I*, or even Hammerstein's earlier work in "Make Believe" from *Show Boat*. "I Have Dreamed" is the kind of sweeping, idealized, romantic song that is at the heart of the Rodgers and Hammerstein output. The arrangement is designed to start with a wispy, tenuous notion, then a tender romantic vision, progressing to full-blown operatic passion.

YOU'RE NEARER is one of Lorenz Hart's typically expressive lyrics in his collaborations with Richard Rodgers. The song was added to the 1940 movie version of the 1939 Rodgers and Hart musical *Too Many Girls*, and was later included in the 1959 revised stage version of *Babes and Arms*. Hart combines genuinely lyrical ideas—"Dearer than the rain is to the earth below, precious as the sun to the things that grow"—with the light touch that keeps the sentiments sincere, but witty, modern and casual, in lines such as "nearer than the ivy to the wall is." I call such spots in American standards "smile lines." Most present day artists sing standards far too earnestly, and miss the playful casual wit found even in the best love songs of the 1920s to mid-1950s. The high point of "You're Nearer" strays furthest away, at the words "Leave me." My arrangement was inspired by Judy Garland's performance on her album "Live at Carnegie Hall," accompanied in a lovely, simple arrangement.

I AM IN LOVE, from the 1953 musical *Can-Can*, is a good example of literate wit mixed with sex that is so typical of many of Cole Porter's lighter love songs. There also seems to be a strong French connection in Porter's material. Five of his Broadway scores, including *Can-Can*, are set in Paris, along with a couple of film scores, and Porter spent a good bit of his life there. A hot, debonaire, urbane Parisian attitude about romance figures into the pallet. This song illustrates the seemingly effortless play of a brilliant creative mind, and I have tried to capture the fun of the song in my arrangement. I can recommend trying some kind of thick, broad French or Italian accent for the repeat of the "bridge" (at the words "I knew the gods were against me…"), snapping out of the accent at "I may lose, but I refuse…"

I CONCENTRATE ON YOU, written for the movie *Broadway Melody of 1940*, was known to me for many years primarily through Frank Sinatra's breezy swing recording from the 1950s. It wasn't until I heard other singers' renditions (Ella Fitzgerald most significantly) that I realized that this is one of the straight-faced love ballads by Cole Porter. The songwriter was able to come up with clever and witty songs fairly easily, but by all accounts, longed most to write powerfully memorable, heartfelt love songs such as Berlin's "What'll I Do?" or "Always."

I HATE YOU, DARLING is from Cole Porter's 1941 show *Let's Face It*. It was originally performed in a quiet and romantic style, making an ironic contrast with the lyrics. I heard the hint of darker emotions in the tune and words, and decided to do a setting taking the love/hate emotions of the song more literally. There is a more explicit reference to sex and relationships in Cole Porter songs than in the work of any other songwriters of the era. Running with that spirit, I stretched the subtext, arranging it as a world-weary Berlin ballad, modeled after Brecht and Weill, where the singer self-mockingly reveals his/her self-destructive liason with someone of inescapable lure.

THEY CAN'T TAKE THAT AWAY FROM ME is one of several songs the Gershwin brothers wrote for Fred Astaire, this one for the 1937 film *Shall We Dance*. It's tucked into the movie in an understated scene on board the Staten Island Ferry, sung once through to Ginger Rogers, without reprise or dancing. The subject is a sophisticated, civil end to romance, and I have tried to evoke that sad nostalgia in the arrangement. Believe it or not, I used sections of *Der Rosenkavalier* as a musical inspiration. Then there is a mid-song shift to a swing style that is an extroverted re-enactment of the romance's bright moments, spilling into a hint of bitterness and desperation ("The way you hold your knife"), concluding with a return to the nostalgia of the opening.

NICE WORK IF YOU CAN GET IT, like all the Gershwin songs in this collection, is from the brothers' late Hollywood work of 1937. This one comes from another Fred Astaire picture, *A Damsel in Distress, sans* Ginger Rogers. Like some of the best lyrics of the late 1930s, this song primarily presents a casual view of romance that masks inner earnest longing. The aesthetics of the best popular music of the era leaned toward a distinctly American style that valued a literate wit, gentle self-deprecation, concealment of effort, indirect references, avoidance of seriousness but with sincere underlying intent, and intelligence expressed in vernacular slang. In this arrangement I have attempted to contrast the dreamy lines with the more rhythmic realism of the song's title phrase. The concealed loneliness and longing emerges at the end in an "emotional coda."

A FOGGY DAY/LOVE WALKED IN. "A Foggy Day," another Fred Astaire song, was written for the 1937 movie *A Damsel in Distress*. In a mere two minutes, the song paints a detailed picture of a lonely American in London (it never states he's an American, but we know it by implication and style), weary of sightseeing, absently roaming the strange city in a grey mood to match the foggy streets. Suddenly and unexpectedly he turns the corner to find love and romance. It's a stunning song. "Love Walked In" was written for the 1937 movie *The Goldwyn Follies*, George Gershwin's last project, sung by by the sweet "lunch counter tenor" of Kenny Baker. I heard the similar sentiments of the two songs, and felt they would comment upon one another if combined in an arrangement.

LOVE IS HERE TO STAY, from the movie *The Goldwyn Follies*, is the last song the Gershwin brothers wrote together, and they certainly never wrote a better popular song. It's intelligent, urbane, casual, witty, undeniably American, and truly romantic—a jewel-like souvenir from 1937 that perfectly represents is era and yet has a timelessness about it. The song is a masterpiece of its style and, in my opinion, has few peers among romantic American ballads.

# THE SWEETEST SOUNDS

Lyrics and Music by Richard Rodgers
Arranged by Richard Walters

ev - er know    Are wait - ing

to    be    said._____    The

most    en - tranc - ing    sight    of    all    Is

yet    for    me    to    see._____

The kind - est words I'll ev - er

know Are wait - ing to be said. _____

The most en - tranc - ing sight of

all Is yet for me to see. _____

And the dear - est love in all the

# I HAVE DREAMED

Words by Oscar Hammerstein II
Music by Richard Rodgers
Arranged by Richard Walters

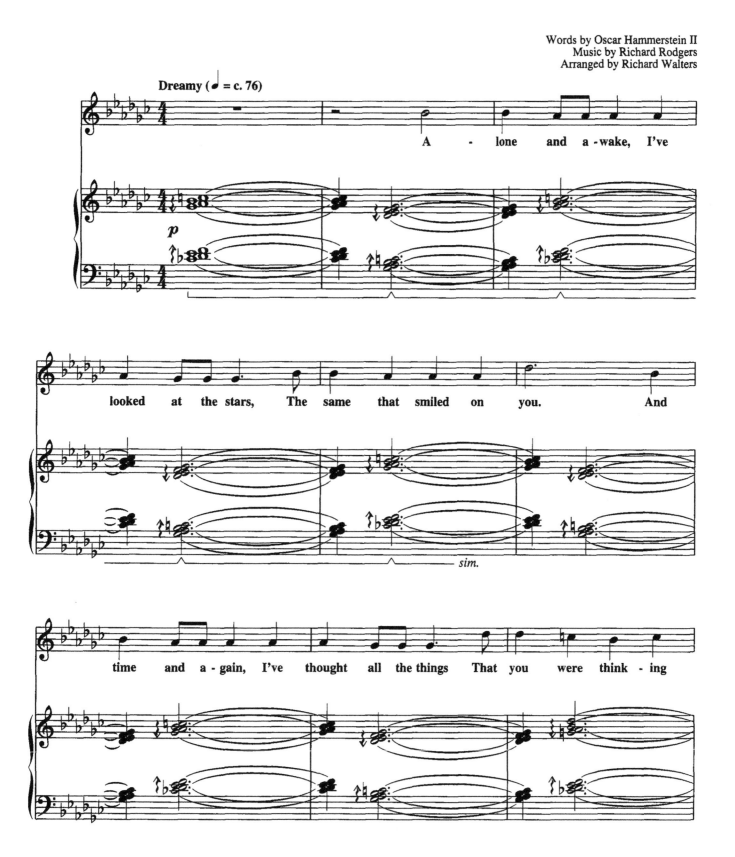

too.

♩ = c. 80-84

I have dreamed

that your arms are love - ly,

I have dreamed what a joy you'll be.

I have dreamed ev - 'ry word you'll

and en - joyed the view. In these

dreams I've loved you so That by now I think I

know What it's like to be loved by

you, I will

love          be - ing  loved     by    you.

I          have dreamed _____ ev -'ry word   you'll _____

whis - per    When    you're ___    close,

close    to ___    me. ___

How    you    look ___    in    the glow    of ___    eve -

*cresc.*

*f    mf    romantically;    think Rachmaninoff in this section*

*loco*

- ning,    I    have    dreamed, ___

and en-joyed the view. In these

dreams I've loved you so That by now I think I

know What it's like to be loved by

you. I will

love   be - ing   loved   by _____ you. _____

# YOU'RE NEARER

Words by Lorenz Hart
Music by Richard Rodgers
Arranged by Richard Walters

Dear - er_____ than the rain is _____ to the earth be -

low, Pre-cious as the sun to the things that

grow. You're near - er_____ than the i - vy_____ to the wall is,

Leave me, but when you're a - way You'll

know _____ you're ___ near - er, _____

rit., ad lib. a tempo

colla voce a tempo

for I love you so. _____

rit.

# I AM IN LOVE

Words and Music by Cole Porter
Arranged by Richard Walters

cy - a -nide          or    or - der cham - pagne?

Oh,   what   is   this   sud - den   jolt?__          I   feel   like   a

fright-ened   colt __          just   hit   by   a   thun - der - bolt;__

I    am    in    love!                    I

lose, but I re - fuse to fight the fire!

So, come and en - light - en my days and nev - er de -

part. You on - ly can bright - en the blaze____

____ that burns in my heart, For I am

wild - ly in love with you

and so in need of __ a stam-pede of __ love! __

I knew the odds _____ were a-

gainst me be-fore, I had no flare _____

for flam-ing de - sire,
But since the gods _____ gave me you to a - dore,
I may lose, but I re - fuse to fight the
fire! _____ So,

*cresc.*

*molto rit.*

*rit.*

*f*

*molto rit.*

*colla voce*

# I CONCENTRATE ON YOU

Words and Music by Cole Porter
Arranged by Richard Walters

Andante espressivo

When - ev - er skies look grey to me _____ And trou - ble be - gins to brew, _____

On your smile so sweet, so ten - der, _____ When at first *{ my kiss you de - cline, / your kiss I de - cline, } On the light in your eyes, When { you / I } sur -

* Traditionally, women sing "your kiss I decline."

ren - der          And once a - gain          our

arms          in - ter - twine. _____

And    so when    wise    men    say    to    me _____

That    love's    young    dream    nev - er    comes

true, _____ To prove that

e - ven wise men can be wrong,

*espressivo*

I con - cen - trate on _____ you.

*etc.*

*This spot might work better for some singers as a subito forte.*

# I HATE YOU, DARLING

Words and Music by Cole Porter
Arranged by Richard Walters

you so.

I should be clev - er and say "good - bye,"

Good - bye, for - ev - er, my but - ter - fly.

But why be clev - er When dar - ling I

darling     And yet I love     you

so.

*Fall off the note.*

# THEY CAN'T TAKE THAT AWAY FROM ME

Words by Ira Gershwin
Music by George Gershwin
Arranged by Richard Walters

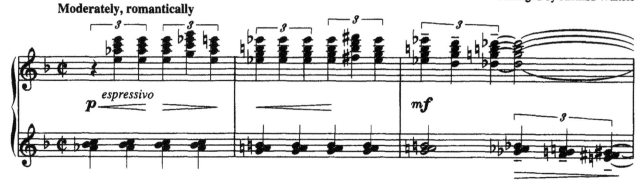

song is end - ed, but as the song - writ - er wrote, The

mel - o - dy ___ lin - gers on. They may take you from

me, (loco) I'll miss your fond ca - ress. But

though they take you from me, I'll still pos - sess:

50

Andante espressivo, rubato

The way you wear your hat, _____

The way you sip your tea, _____ The mem-'ry of all that. _____

No, no! They can't _____ take that a - way _____ from me!

The way your smile just beams, _____

*These optional notes may be played to support the singer's entrances.

The way you sing off - key, ___

The way you haunt my dreams. ___

No, no! They can't ___ take that a - way ___ from me. ___

We may nev - er, _____ nev - er meet a - gain ___ on the

bump - y road to love, ___ Still I'll al - ways, _____ al - ways

keep the mem - 'ry of ____

The way you hold your knife, ____

The way we danced till three, ____

The way you've changed my life. ____

No, no! They can't ____ take that a - way ____ from me! ____ No! ____ They

No, __ no! __ They can't __ take that a - way from me. We may

**Faster and freely, parlando**
**Swing beat stops, straight eighths**

nev - er, nev - er meet a - gain on the bump - y road to

love, Still I'll al - ways, al - ways keep the mem - 'ry

of _____

The way you hold___ your knife,___

The way we danced___ till three,___

The way you've changed___ my life.___

# NICE WORK IF YOU CAN GET IT

Words by Ira Gershwin
Music by George Gershwin
Arranged by Richard Walters

get it if____ you try.____ Just im - ag - ine

some - one____ Wait - ing at the cot - tage door, ____

Where two hearts be - come one____ Who could ask for an - y -thing more?__

Lov - ing one who loves you, And then tak - ing that

vow, Nice work__ if you can get it, And if you

get it,_____ Won't__ you tell me how?__

*f hard swing rhythm*

*p legato*

* The singer may improvise any syllables to create the dreamy effect if a hum is not preferred.

And then tak - ing that vow,

Nice work if you can get it,

And if you get it, Won't you tell __ me

Opt.

how?

*quick to the end*

# A FOGGY DAY/LOVE WALKED IN

Words by Ira Gershwin
Music by George Gershwin
Arranged by Richard Walters

had me down. ___ I viewed the morn-ing

with a-larm, ___ The Brit-ish Mu-se-um had

lost its charm. ___ How long, I won-dered, could

this thing last? ___ But the age of mir-a-cles

had - n't passed, ___ For, sud - den - ly, ___ I

saw you there, ___ And through fog - gy Lon - don

town the sun was shin - ing ___ ev - 'ry -

where. Love ___

L'istesso tempo

*Some singers may be more comfortable with a forte here.*

lo," Though not a word was spo - ken. One

look and I for - got the gloom of the past;

One look and I had found my fu - ture at

last. One look and I had found a world__

and my heart seemed to know That love said "Hel-
lo," Though not a word was spo-ken.
One look and I for-got the gloom of the past;
One look and I had found my fu-ture at last.

One look and I had found a world com-plete-ly new, When love walked in with you.

*Expressively fall off the note.

# LOVE IS HERE TO STAY

Words by Ira Gershwin
Music by George Gershwin
Arranged by Richard Walters

way.

In time the Rock - ies may crum - ble, Gi -

cresc.

mf    mp

bral - ter may tum - ble,

They're on - ly made of clay,

But

our love is here to stay.

p cresc.

**A little freely and faster, parlando**

The more I read the pa - pers, The less I com - pre - hend The

mf    mp